The King's Pilgrimage

The King's Pilgrimage

An Account of King George V's Visit to the
War Graves in Belgium and France

"Their Name Liveth For Evermore"

Third Millennium
Publishing

First published in 1922 by Hodder and Stoughton Ltd, London

This edition published in Great Britain in 2018 by
Third Millennium Publishing (an imprint of Profile Books Ltd)
3 Holford Yard
Bevin Way
London WC1X 9HD
United Kingdom

www.tmbooks.com

A CIP catalogue record for this book is available from the British Library.

ISBN 9781788160971

Printed and bound in Great Britain by Clays, St Ives plc

Introduction

IT was the wish of King George V to honour the dead of the Great War by visiting the Military cemeteries in Belgium and France as soon as this were practically possible.

He determined that the visit should be simple and dignified, with the minimum of formality and trappings.

Thus it was, following the first State visit to Belgium in 1922, that he assembled a small but distinguished party to accompany him:

Field Marshal the Earl Haig, The Rt. Hon. Sir Frederick Ponsonby, Major General Sir Fabian Ware, Colonel Clive Wigram and Major Reginald Seymour.

They were joined by Queen Mary, Lady Haig (her Lady-in-Waiting) and Admiral of the Fleet the Earl Beatty towards the end of the itinerary.

Frank Fox, War Correspondent for the *Morning Post* at the time of the German invasion of Belgium in 1914, had subsequently been commissioned as a combatant and was seriously wounded on the Somme.

After convalescence, during which he worked for MI7, he joined Haig's GHQ in Montreuil-sur-Mer. His name probably came to the fore to write this narrative of the King's Pilgrimage, through his association with Ware on the *Morning Post*, before the latter championed the formation of the Imperial War Graves Commission.

The result is this book, full of evocative and unposed photographs, preceded by Rudyard Kipling's verse. It is being republished to mark the Centenary of the 1918 Armistice.

Dr Charles Goodson-Wickes, DL
Great-Grandson and Literary Executor of Sir Frank Fox, OBE

May 1922.

I am interested to hear of the proposed
publication of the record of my pilgrimage to the
War Graves.

It grieves me to think how many relatives
are prevented from visiting the graves of their
dear ones through lack of means. During my recent
visit to the Cemeteries in France and Belgium, I
was glad to learn that various organisations are
endeavouring to meet this difficulty by raising
funds which I trust will be substantially assisted
by the sale of the book.

George R.I.

The King's Pilgrimage

OUR King went forth on pilgrimage
    His prayer and vows to pay
To them that saved our Heritage
    And cast their own away.
And there was little show of pride,
    Or prows of belted steel,
For the clean-swept oceans every side
    Lay free to every keel.

And the first land he found, it was shoal
        and banky ground
    Where the broader seas begin,
And a pale tide grieving at the broken
        harbour mouth
    Where they worked the Death Ships in;
And there was neither gull on the wing,
    Nor wave that could not tell
Of the bodies that were buckled in the
        lifebuoy's ring
    That slid from swell to swell.

All that they had they gave – they gave;
    and they shall not return,
For these are those that have no grave
    where any heart may mourn.

And the next land he found, it was low
        and hollow ground
    Where once the cities stood,
But the man-high thistle had been
        master of it all,
    Or the bulrush by the flood;
And there was neither blade of grass
    Nor lone star in the sky,
But shook to see some spirit pass
    And took its agony.

And the next land he found, it was bare
        and hilly ground
    Where once the bread-corn grew,
But the fields were cankered and the
        water was defiled,
    And the trees were riven through;
And there was neither paved highway,
    Nor secret path in the wood,
But had borne its weight of the broken clay,
    And darkened 'neath the blood.

Father and Mother they put aside, and
        the nearer love also —
An hundred thousand men who died whose
        grave shall no man know.

THE KING'S PILGRIMAGE

And the last land he found, it was fair
    and level ground
      Above a carven Stone,
And a stark Sword brooding on the
    bosom of the Cross
      Where high and low are one;
And there was grass and the living trees,
    And the flowers of the Spring,
And there lay gentlemen from out of
    all the seas
      That ever called him King.

Twixt Nieuport sands and the eastward lands
    where the Four Red Rivers spring,
Five hundred thousand gentlemen of those that
    served their King.

All that they had they gave – they gave –
    In sure and single faith.
There can no knowledge reach the grave
    To make them grudge their death
Save only if they understood
    That, after all was done
We they redeemed denied their blood,
    And mocked the gains it won.

RUDYARD KIPLING

I : *"Our King went forth on pilgrimage"*

IT was our King's wish that he should go as a private pilgrim, with no trappings of state nor pomp of ceremony, and with only a small suite, to visit the tombs in Belgium and France of his comrades who gave up their lives in the Great War. In the uniform which they wore on service, he passed from one to another of the cemeteries which, in their noble simplicity, express perfectly the proud grief of the British race in their dead; and, at the end, within sight of the white cliffs of England, spoke his thoughts in a message of eloquence which moved all his Empire to sympathy.

The Governments of France and of Belgium, our allies in the war for the freedom of the world, respected the King's wish. Nowhere did official ceremony intrude on an office of private devotion. But nothing could prevent the people of the countryside gathering around the places which the King visited, bringing with them flowers, and joining their tribute to his. They acclaimed him not so much as King, but rather as the head of those khaki columns which crossed the Channel to help to guard their homes; in their minds the memory of the glad relief of August 1914, when they learnt that the British were with them in the war and felt that the ultimate end was secure. Many of them were of the peasants who, before the scattered graves of our dead had been gathered into enduring cemeteries, had graced them with flowers, making vases of shell-cases gathered from the battlefields. The King was deeply moved by their presence, at seeing them leave for an hour the task of building up their ruined homes and shattered farms, and coming with pious gratitude to share his homage to the men who had been faithful to their trust unto death. To those around him he spoke more than once in thankful appreciation of this good feeling of the people of France and Belgium. Especially was he pleased to see the children of the countryside crowd around him, and when little choirs of them sang "God Save the King" in quaintly accented words his feeling was manifest.

There came thus to the pilgrimage from the first an atmosphere of affectionate intimacy between these people who were not his subjects and the British King. They gathered around him as around a friend, the old women leaning forward to catch his words, the children trying to come close enough to touch him, seeing in his uniform again the "Tommy" who had proved such a gentle soul when he came for a brief rest from the horrors of the battle-field to the villages behind the line and helped "mother" with the housework and nursed the baby. At one village a gendarme, feeling in his official soul that this was really no way to treat a King, tried to arrange some more formal atmosphere. But in vain. The villagers saw the old friendly good-humoured British Army back in France, and could not be official.

Now and then at a cemetery the King met relatives, in some cases from far-off Pacific Dominions, visiting their dead, and he stopped to speak with them because they were on the same mission as he was, of gratitude and reverence. One mother, moved by the kindness of the

King's greeting, opened her heart to him and told, with the simple eloquence of real feeling, how she had just come from her son's grave and was proud that he had died for his King and country; that every care had been taken to find and identify it, and "more could not have been done if it had been the Prince of Wales himself."

At several points the workers of the Imperial War Graves Commission – practically all of whom had gone through the campaign, and now are reverently and carefully tending the last resting-places of their fallen comrades – assembled to greet the King. He spoke with them also, giving them thanks for their work and noting their war medals and asking them about their life in the camps, or with the mobile caravans which, in the districts where housing cannot yet be found, move from cemetery to cemetery, keeping fresh the tribute of grass and flowers and trees – caravans which bring back vividly one's memory of the old British supply columns, for they are almost invariably led by a small self-important and well-fed dog.

When at Vlamertinghe – where are the graves of the first Dominion soldiers who fell in the war – the High Commissioner for Canada, the Hon. P. C. Larkin, was met visiting the Canadian graves there; the King gave him a very warm greeting. He showed that there is never absent from his mind the thought that in the greatest Ordeal of Battle which the British race has had to pass through, the children nations of his Empire came to the side of the Mother Country, with the instinctive spontaneity of the blood in a limb responding to a message from the heart; and that the crimson tie of kinship never broke nor slackened through all the perilous anxious years. Across the sea, held for them as a safe path by the Navy, the men of the Empire – and the women, too – kept passing at the King's word to whatsoever point at which the peril was greatest, the work most exacting. The graves of the Flanders battlefields told triumphantly of this august Imperial assembly – the dead of the Mother Country having around them those of India, Canada, Australia, New Zealand, South Africa, Newfoundland, the West Indies, the Pacific Islands.* At every point the voices of the dead bespoke, in the King's words, "the single-hearted assembly of nations and races which form our Empire."

◆　　◆　　◆　　◆　　◆

It was at the close of a State visit to the King of the Belgians that the King left Brussels on a special train early on the morning of May 11th. The King lived on the train (in his own carriage which had been in France throughout the war) during the tour, motor-cars meeting it at fixed halting-places for the visits to the cemeteries. He was accompanied by Field-Marshal Earl Haig, whom His Majesty specially wished to be at his side on this pilgrimage. The Royal party was a small one; in addition to Lord Haig, it consisted of Major-General Sir Fabian Ware (who, as Vice-Chairman of the Imperial War Graves Commission, was in charge of all the arrangements) and of three members of the suite, the Rt. Hon. Sir Frederick Ponsonby, Colonel Clive Wigram, and Major R. Seymour. The first visit paid was to Zeebrugge Churchyard, where

---

* The total number of the dead of the British Empire in the Great War was recently officially stated in the House of Commons to be 946,023, distributed as follows: Great Britain and Ireland, 743,702; Canada, Australia, New Zealand, South Africa, Newfoundland, Colonies, 140,923; India, 61,398.

rest some of those who fell in the Zeebrugge Battle which marked St. George's Day, 1918. Many of the graves are still unidentified, but, with the aid of enemy burial lists recently secured, it is hoped that the identity of some, at any rate, will be established. There was, by the King's express wish, no formal ceremony at this nor any other cemetery before Terlincthun, but the schoolchildren of Zeebrugge assembled and sang the British National Anthem and brought flowers for the graves.

The King went on to examine the scene of the exploit of *Vindictive* and her supporting ships. The day was bright and breezy, and, by a happy chance, a Belgian fishing fleet was making for harbour with the night's harvest of the sea. To the eye of the sailor this gave clear indication of the lay of the harbour approaches and of its entrance, and helped materially to illustrate the way in which the Mole was approached and the task with which the British naval forces were faced. The King took the keenest interest in every detail of the exploit and of the tactics employed. He stayed for some time at the point where the submarine, loaded with high explosives, rammed the Mole to breach it, with the double object of cutting off the enemy garrison on the Mole from reinforcements and of helping the obstacles which were to be sunk in the fairway to silt up the harbour by letting in the drifting sands. The positions where the ships were sunk in the fairway were examined, and the King, with his professional knowledge of the Service in which he spent his young manhood, could reconstruct the whole battle. He made particular inspection of the spot where the landing party from *Vindictive* scaled the Mole – perhaps the most astonishing "boarding" feat of naval history.

With some reluctance the King turned his back to the sea, and the Royal party went on by train to Zonnebeke. Here the party left the train and proceeded by car to visit Tyne Cot Cemetery, which is in the midst of what was the most desolate and terrible of all battlefields – the Passchendaele marshes. Tyne Cot (or cottage) was on the north side of the Ypres-Roulers railway, near the village of Passchendaele. It was here that the enemy first built their "pill boxes" or concrete forts. The waterlogged ground would not allow of the construction of dug-outs nor of effective shelter trenches, and the enemy sought to hold their line with these strong points of reinforced concrete, heavily armed with machine guns, to attack which the British storming infantry often had to wade waist-deep in mire up to the very muzzles of the guns.

No part of the long trench line which stretched from the sea to Switzerland has such shuddering memories for the British Army as Passchendaele. There it had the problem of storming a whole series of miniature Zeebrugge Moles standing in seas of slimy mud, to sink into which from the narrow built paths of trench-boards was to perish. Of the nine thousand British soldiers buried in Tyne Cot Cemetery, over six thousand are "unknown". The hateful mud swallowed up their identity with their lives.

Many places on the long trench line which stretched like a dreadful scar across Belgium and France the King knew during the days of the war. Very jealously the secrets of his visits to the Front had to be guarded then, especially when both the King and the Heir Apparent were at the same time in the battle-line; and no public record exists of them. But it is safe to say that Tyne Cot he saw for the first time this May afternoon. He understood how appalling was the task which his soldiers faced there, and, turning to the great "pill box" which still stands in the middle of the cemetery, he said that it should never be moved, should remain always as a monument to the heroes whose graves stood thickly around. From its roof he gazed sadly over the sea of wooden crosses, a "massed multitude of silent witnesses to the desolation of war." It is indeed fitting that this should form, as it will, the foundation for the great Cross of Sacrifice shortly to be built up as a central memorial in this cemetery.

ZEEBRUGGE

ARRIVAL AT THE MOLE

ZEEBRUGGE

INSPECTING THE MOLE

ZEEBRUGGE

AT THE BREACH IN THE MOLE

ZEEBRUGGE CHURCHYARD

INSPECTING BRITISH GRAVES

AT BRANDHOEK MILITARY CEMETERY

TYNE COT CEMETERY

THE KING AND THE GARDENERS

TYNE COT CEMETERY

TYNE COT CEMETERY

THE KING READING INSCRIPTIONS ON WOODEN CROSSES

TYNE COT CEMETERY

INSPECTING THE GERMAN BLOCKHOUSE WHICH WILL
FORM THE BASE OF THE CENTRAL MEMORIAL

YPRES TOWN CEMETERY

THE GRAVE OF H.H. PRINCE MAURICE OF BATTENBERG

YPRES TOWN CEMETERY

MENIN GATE, YPRES

EXAMINING THE PLANS FOR THE MEMORIAL TO
THOSE WHO HAVE NO KNOWN GRAVE

VLAMERTINGHE MILITARY CEMETERY

VLAMERTINGHE MILITARY CEMETERY

THE BURGOMASTER'S DAUGHTER PRESENTING A WREATH

Our King went forth on pilgrimage
His prayer and vows to pay
To them that saved our heritage
And cast their own away.

*"I have been on a solemn pilgrimage in honour
of a people who died for all free men"*

II: *"It was low and hollow ground where once the cities stood"*

THE King's route after leaving Tyne Cot Cemetery brought him to the salient where the British Army held Ypres as the gate guarding the Channel ports. The enemy rush to Paris had failed, and he was seeking a way to victory by a rush to seize the French side of the English Channel as a prelude to the invasion of England. In the first Battle of Ypres the enemy sought with enormous superiority of numbers to overwhelm the British force which barred the Calais Road. To hold Ypres was vital, and yet Ypres was, humanly speaking, indefensible, within a saucer-shaped salient dominated on three sides by the German artillery.

The attack was pushed on with fierce energy from October 21st 1914 onwards, and was met with heroic stubbornness by a woefully thin khaki line. At one stage there was no question of reliefs. Every man practically in the British Force, including cooks and batmen, was in the front line, and these men held to the trenches day after day, night after night, without sleep, with little food, with no intermission from rifle and shellfire.

During the second Battle of Ypres, in the spring of 1915, the war took on a new phase with the enemy use of asphyxiating gas as a weapon. Of this odious and unexpected form of warfare the Canadians were the first victims, but withstood the surprise with a cool heroism which saved the day.

There were other battles of Ypres, and all the land around was saturated with the blood of heroes. So this "low and hollow ground," stiffened with our dead, is holy soil to the British race. The King chose fitly to render there his homage to the dead of the Belgian Army who on the Yser held the left flank of the line through all the years of bitter fighting for Ypres.

On his way to the Menin Gate of Ypres city, the King directed the cars to turn aside to the Town Cemetery, that he might stand silent for a few moments by the graves of Prince Maurice of Battenberg, Lord Charles Mercer-Nairne, Major the Hon. W. Cadogan, and other officers, some of those of his own personal friends whom the war claimed, and whose graves lie among those of their men, marked by the same simple memorials.

◆   ◆   ◆   ◆   ◆

Ypres today is no longer a mass of shell-shattered ruins. The work of reconstruction has been carried on earnestly, and thousands of new houses have been built. But nothing can ever restore the mediaeval beauty of the city which grew like a noble wood in carved stone on the Flanders Plain. The ruins of the Cloth Hall will remain as the monument of the old city which was once a world's capital for those who wove wool into fine cloth. The old ramparts at the Menin Gate – stout walls which provided security for the British signallers even in the most furious bombardments – will remain as another monument, an effective symbol of the British Army at Ypres, very sorely battered, but still holding secure.

It is proposed by the Imperial War Graves Commission that at the Menin Gate there should be a memorial to those of the Empire's Armies who fell in this area but have no known graves. It will crown these ramparts with a great double arch, enclosing a vaulted hall, in which will be recorded the names of all those lost in the neighbouring battlefields whose bodies have not been recovered and identified. The design provides that the arch facing Menin, where once the foe was drawn up, will be surmounted by the great figure of a lion alert in defence, the arch facing Ypres by some other symbolical sculpture.

◆   ◆   ◆   ◆   ◆

The King was met at the Menin Gate by representatives of the Belgian Government and Army, by Major Michelet and M. Lorel of the Belgian Graves Services, and by the Burgomaster of Ypres. The industrious rebuilders of Ypres paused from their work for an hour and assembled to give him a hearty greeting. The King entrusted a chaplet of palms and bay leaves with a spray of red roses in memory of the Belgian dead to Major Michelet. He then congratulated the Burgomaster on the progress his citizens were making with the work of reconstruction. Sir Reginald Blomfield, architect of the memorial at the Menin Gate, submitted to the King the designs and plans of the monument. His Majesty emphasised the need that the names inscribed should be clear to all to read.

◆   ◆   ◆   ◆   ◆

Leaving the Menin Gate, the King passed by the ruins of the Cloth Hall and of the Cathedral, noting the irreparable loss to the world through the destruction of these magnificent examples of Flemish architecture. It was observed that the drivers found it somewhat difficult to find a way through the new Ypres which is growing up under the industrious hands of the Belgian population. Ypres, the "Museum City" of 1914, is known to many. The "Wipers" of 1918, a tumble of desolation through which the soldiers passed under constant shellfire by burrowed paths, became familiar to almost every British regiment. But this new, rebuilding Ypres is a stranger.

The route of the pilgrimage went from Ypres to Vlamertinghe, passing on the way the British cemetery behind Ypres Reservoir, the Asylum British Cemetery, the cemetery on the Dickebusch Road, and the Railway Chateau Cemetery. At Vlamertinghe Military Cemetery the King stopped and, as has already been noted, visited the Canadian graves with the High Commissioner for Canada, as well as paying his tribute to the many British buried there. This cemetery, between Poperinghe and Ypres, was begun by the French troops, then holding part of the line here. It contains 1,114 graves of British soldiers, 52 of Canadian, 4 of Australian, 2 of South African, 2 of soldiers of the Royal Newfoundland Regiment, one of an Indian soldier, and one of an unknown soldier. Very many of the British graves are of Territorial dead. There are, for example, nearly 250 Lancashire Territorials buried there: those splendid men who proved, both in Gallipoli and France, that the town-bred population of the Mother Country was fit, in courage and endurance, to rank with the historic regiments of the line and with the young giants from the Oversea Dominions.

◆ ◆ ◆ ◆ ◆

From Vlamertinghe, along the granite-set roads which were for years pounded by our ammunition wagons and supply trains, but the dust arising from which now proclaims the works of peace as the country-folk drive their carts loaded with bricks and timber for rebuilding, the King went on to the Hop Store Cemetery, greeted everywhere with cordial sympathy. Hop Store village was used from time to time as headquarters both by our heavy artillery and by our field ambulances. The site of the cemetery is on a marshy patch of ground, but it was drained by the Royal Engineers early in 1917, and recently a moat has been constructed on three sides. It holds 247 of our dead.

From Hop Store the King went on to Brandhoek, which was a comparatively safe area during the war, and therefore a post for field ambulances. The old Military Cemetery, which the King visited, was opened in May 1915 in a field adjoining the Dressing Station, and was closed in July 1917. It shelters the bodies of 601 soldiers from the Home Country, 62 from Canada, 4 from Australia, and 2 of the Bermuda Volunteer Rifle Corps. In July 1917 the Military Cemetery was opened 300 yards away, and in August 1917 a third cemetery was opened.

Poperinghe was next visited. This agricultural town on the road between Ypres and Hazebrouck, situated among hop-fields and dairy farms, was a haven of rest in the early days of the war. Although occasionally bombarded at long range, it was the nearest town to Ypres which was reasonably safe. It was at first a casualty-clearing station centre. Later, in 1916, when shellfire increased, it was decided to move back the casualty-clearing station to a safer zone, and Poperinghe became a field ambulance station. The earliest British graves at Poperinghe are in the Communal Cemetery, a walled graveyard at the entrance to the town. The old Military Cemetery was made in the course of the first Battle of Ypres, and was closed (so far as British burials were concerned) in May 1915. The New Military Cemetery was made in June 1915. It contains the graves of 596 soldiers from the Home Country, 55 from Canada, 20 from Australia, 3 from New Zealand, and 2 of the British West Indies Regiment.

Lijssenthoek was the last of the cemeteries on Belgian soil visited. This cemetery is at Remy Siding, on the south side of the Hazebrouck-Ypres railway line, between Poperinghe and Abeele. The site was first used for burials by a French military hospital, and there is a group of French graves on what is now the eastern boundary of the cemetery. The earliest British burial dates from June 1915. This cemetery had to be repeatedly enlarged as the campaign levied its toll on our forces. It now contains 9,795 British and Dominion graves, 892 French, 2 Belgian, 52 American, and 32 Chinese. The majority of burials took place from the Canadian casualty-clearing stations at Remy. Of the French graves, 10 are those of unknown soldiers and 689 will remain in the cemetery.

◆   ◆   ◆   ◆   ◆

Going out of Belgium to France the sun was shining and the graciousness of Nature, covering with herb and blossom the ulcers of the old battlefields, made this corner of Flanders seem a fair and human country. For those who now saw the district for the first time, the concrete forts lying like the bleached skeletons of strange monsters in the fields, and the serried ranks of the graves, coming up in line after line to give their mute witness, told something of what it cost to hold the Ypres Salient. But the King knew all that it had been in the long dark winters of the war, when the very abomination of desolation brooded over it, and in its pools of slime his soldiers struggled and choked that the fields of England might be kept free of the foe. He did not hide from those with him that the memory of it weighed heavy on him and that in his mind, with pride in the thought of such superhuman devotion, there was a passionate hope that never again in the world's history would men be called upon to suffer as these men had suffered.

Speaking, too, of the cemeteries, where general and private rest side by side beneath the same simple stones, equal in the honour of their death for duty's sake, he agreed that this was the only possible way.

NOTRE DAME DE LORETTE

THE KING MEETING MARSHAL FOCH

NOTRE DAME DE LORETTE

SALUTING THE FRENCH COLOUR PARTY

NOTRE DAME DE LORETTE

SALUTING THE FRENCH COLOUR PARTY

NOTRE DAME DE LORETTE

THE FRENCH GUARD OF HONOUR

NOTRE DAME DE LORETTE

THE KING AND MARSHAL FOCH

NOTRE DAME DE LORETTE

"I have come to lay a wreath in homage on the tombs
of French heroes who have fallen for their country"

NOTRE DAME DE LORETTE

THE SILENCE AND THE SALUTE TO THE DEAD

NOTRE DAME DE LORETTE

THE BROW OF THE HILL OVERLOOKING THE RIDGE

THE KING WITH MARSHAL FOCH, GENERAL WEYGAND
AND FIELD-MARSHAL EARL HAIG

INSPECTION OF GARDENERS

FORCEVILLE CEMETERY

FORCEVILLE

FORCEVILLE

THE KING SPEAKING TO THE MAYOR

LOUVENCOURT

LOUVENCOURT

A TRAVELLING GARDENING PARTY

PICQUIGNY

WHERE A NUMBER OF AUSTRALIANS LIE

CROUY BRITISH CEMETERY

THE KING TALKING TO TWO BEREAVED AUSTRALIAN RELATIVES

III: *"It was bare and hilly ground where once the bread-corn grew"*

IN the evening of May 11th the King passed from Belgium into France on his way to Vimy, which had been chosen as the resting-place for the night. As the train arrived at Hazebrouck, the first stop after crossing the frontier, the Prefect of the Nord, together with the Maire of Hazebrouck, received His Majesty. The Maire (M. L'Abbé Lemire) is a figure known to every soldier who passed through Hazebrouck during the war; not only had he been a constant friend to all ranks of the British Army, but his courageous and imperturbable control of his townspeople during the early days of 1914 will always be remembered in the history of the war. The journey through the stricken area of French Flanders was full of memories of heroic resolution and accomplishment. Those fields yonder were tilled during the war by the French – the old men, women, and children – under the guns of the enemy, the plough-share's orderly cutting of the soil now and again interrupted as exploding shells dug their pits, but the stubborn peasants going on with their toil. Those same fields, later, knew at its best the practical heroism of the British soldier (is not that the dominant characteristic of the British race, its power to bring the highest courage to the common labour of life?). The German onrush had brought areas (which the French had cultivated under shellfire) within the zone of the front line and the civilians had to be sent back. Since every ear of wheat was precious at that time, the British Army organised to save this part of the French harvest, and actually reaped the product of eighteen thousand acres. It was gallant work, chiefly done by fighting men between their turns in the trenches. When an area was under the direct fire and close observation of the enemy the crop was cut at night. When the enemy used gas shells to prevent the work, the soldier reapers went on with their task in gas masks. One area of six acres of corn was so close to the enemy trenches that the idea of saving it seemed desperate. But one night seventeen volunteers with hand scythes cleared the whole of it in the three hours of darkness that were available. This, more perhaps than any deeds done in the heat and ardour of battle, impressed the French farmers and set in their minds an imperishable memory of the gallant friendliness of the British.

◆　　◆　　◆　　◆　　◆

Coming to Vimy and looking out on its ridge, the King bethought of the great battle in which his Canadian troops had won this key position, and telegraphed to Lord Byng, the present Governor-General of Canada, and before in command of the Canadian Corps, the following message of thankfulness and congratulation:

"I have just spent the night at Vimy. My thoughts are with you." It was a right royal remembrance which delighted Canada.

◆　　◆　　◆　　◆　　◆

The first act of the King on May 12th was to pay his homage to the dead of the armies of France, and he passed through the torn and shattered country at its base to Notre Dame de Lorette, the great bastion hill which was the centre of the Allies' resistance in the North. Noticing that his train would pass by it, he had written personally to Marshal Foch asking him to meet him there, so that the great commander might be at his side when he paid his homage.

To the French people Notre Dame de Lorette is *la colline sacrée* of the Great War. It was the key for the defence of Flanders and Artois, the most bitterly contested strong point on French soil, not excepting Verdun. For twelve continuous months, without a day's interruption, one battle raged round the hill. Every yard of its soil bears shell scars and has been dyed with noble blood. Altogether, over 100,000 men gave up their lives around this hallowed hill, and it was the most fitting place for the King to pay his homage to the noble dead of the French Army.

Nor is Notre Dame de Lorette without its proud memories for the British Army, which held for long the Artois line of defences. Hardly one of the many thousands of British officers who served in the Royal Regiment of Artillery during the Great War but who has at one time "observed" for his guns from Lorette. All the batteries, field and heavy, for miles around were directed from the observation posts on the hill, which gave a great range of view, north and south, so far behind the enemy lines that the housing of his balloons and the movements of his railways could be followed.

As it stands today, Lorette has been cleared of much of its timber and is thicketed with the clustering crosses of the French cemeteries. It is intended to erect upon it a memorial to the dead of the Artois and Flanders fronts. The design by M. Louis Cordonnier, an architect of Lille (which was shown by him to the King), provides for a Basilica on the spot where once was built the chapel of Notre Dame de Lorette. One hundred metres from the Basilica will be built a beacon tower which will show a perpetual light visible for fifty miles around, reminding the miner and agriculturist and trader of future generations with what great sacrifice their country was held free.

◆　　◆　　◆　　◆　　◆

The King, reaching Notre Dame de Lorette, walked up the steep slope of the hill to a little plateau, in the centre of the thickly clustered French graves, where he was met by Marshal Foch, General Weygand (the Marshal's Chief of Staff), General Lacapelle, commanding the First Army Corps, and M. Cauzel, Prefect of the Pas-de-Calais.

"I have come," said the King as he took Marshal Foch by the hand, "to lay a wreath in homage on the tombs of French heroes who have fallen for their country."

The trumpets sounded a salute as the King arrived and inspected the French Guard of Honour, and then with Marshal Foch he walked along the lines of white wooden crosses of the cemetery.

The King came back to the centre of the hill, where will be erected the memorial to the dead, and, addressing Marshal Foch, said: "I am happy, M. le Marechal, that you are by my side at this moment, when I come to place this wreath in deserved homage to the heroic soldiers of

France." On a mound over which flew the French flag he placed his chaplet of red roses, palm and bay, bearing the simple inscription, "From King George V,—12th May, 1922," then stood for two minutes silent at the salute, Marshal Foch and Field-Marshal Earl Haig on either side.

Deeply moved was the King and those around him. All the tragedy and all the heroism which Notre Dame de Lorette symbolises rose up before the mind. At the King's feet stretched, in row after row, the tombs of the French, who lost almost a complete generation of their glorious youth in defence of their country. Beyond the line of tombs showed for miles and miles devastated France – the ruins which had been great manufacturing towns, the wastes which had been fertile fields, the dusty stains on the landscape which had been smiling villages, the tangles of splintered stumps which had been fruitful trees. Here was the record of the scientifically considered, the systematically prepared, the meticulously executed ruin of France; and these graves were of those who stemmed the wave of that hideous desolation.

Leaving the cemetery and walking on a little distance, the King, Marshal Foch, and Earl Haig took their stand on a commanding point of the hill and discussed the strategy of the campaign. Marshal Foch and Earl Haig talked over some of the great actions of the war, pointing out to the King various points the names of which are household words today – Souchez, Vimy, the Labyrinth, Loos, Lens, and those betraying dumps of the coal pits which caused the loss of so many a soldier.

The King listened with keen interest and was clearly delighted at the cordial comradeship of the two great soldiers. He turned to them at one point with the confident query: *"Toujours bons amis, n'est-ce pas?"* Marshal Foch replied with fervour: *"Toujours, toujours, pour les mêmes causes et les mêmes raisons,"* and grasped Earl Haig's hand. As the two Marshals clasped hands in the grip of comradeship the King placed his hand over theirs.

A scene to be remembered for all time, the making of that pledge and its sealing with the King's hand on the sacred hill of Notre Dame de Lorette.

Leaving the hill, the King and his party proceeded by car in the direction of Albert, going through the mining villages, still mostly ruins, but busy now again with useful industry. The route followed passed such well-known places as Souchez and Mont St. Eloy. The day being a crowded one, there was no time to stop in the ruined town of Arras, but with the thought which characterised all the arrangements which the French had made, the Prefect had detailed a guard of cyclists to meet the cars at the entrance to the town. They conducted the King's car through Arras, passing all the chief points in the town which had suffered from the enemy's fire.

From thence the King went on to Bapaume, Warlencourt, and Le Sars, seeing again the Somme battlefield, the scene of the first great British offensive attack in the summer of 1916. It was there the New Armies were put to the crucial test and proved that they were worthy to take up and guard the tradition of the old Regular Army. In many hundreds of thousands of British homes today the Battle of the Somme is the greatest memory of the campaign, for it marked the end of the wearisome trench war, the first move to drive the enemy from out of the land he had invaded, though he had made of it, as he thought, an invincible fortress. They can remember the joy they had in the heartening roar of our guns as they prepared the attack, the multitudinous clamour of the field guns, the sharp scream of the 12-inch guns which reared their monstrous throats by street corners of Albert, the deep note, as of a giant's cough, of the 15-inch howitzers, pushing out shells as big almost as mines.

Bitter was the fighting on the Somme, most bitter when in moving to the attack the infantry encountered rain and the chalky downs became as grease under their feet. But there was the exultant feeling of advancing, of winning back day by day a little bit of France. The Somme heartened the British soldier with the knowledge that impregnableness had lost its meaning, heartened them, too, with the knowledge that our Air Force had won supremacy in the air, and now could blind the enemy at will by driving his aeroplanes and observation balloons out of the sky.

Passing by several cemeteries and battle exploit memorials erected by both home and Dominion units, the party reached Albert, from the ruined cathedral tower of which a great statue of the Virgin and Child hung perilously through years of the war. It was said that, when it fell, the war would end; and in truth it did not fall until the end was near. A halt at Albert had not been arranged, but the King, noting a party of workers of the War Graves Commission in a camp there, stopped and talked with the men.

The afternoon was occupied in visiting cemeteries in the surrounding districts.

◆   ◆   ◆   ◆   ◆

For the Somme victories we paid a heavy price, as the crowding Somme cemeteries show. The King visited of these:

WARLENCOURT. This cemetery is 500 yards north of the Butte de Warlencourt, across the Albert-Bapaume road. It is entirely a concentration cemetery, begun towards the end of 1919. It includes the graves brought from the original cemeteries at Hexham Road, Le Sars, and Seven Elms, Flers, as well as over 3,000 British graves due to the fighting which took place around the Butte de Warlencourt from the autumn of 1916 to the spring of 1917, and again in the German advance and retreat of 1918.

WARLOY-BAILLON. There are two cemeteries at the village of that name. The Communal Cemetery is on the east of the village and the Extension is in an apple orchard on the eastern side of the cemetery. The apple trees around the graves, in blossom on this spring day, made the burial ground very beautiful. All the cemeteries of France and Belgium have in common a noble simplicity of design, but each one has some particular feature. One is beautiful with orchard trees; another is graced with rose trees; of another sentinel poplars are a feature; of another the shroud-like cypresses. In every case the planning of a cemetery, its alignment, the site of the Cross of Sacrifice, and the Stone of Remembrance, its plantations and walls, are designed by the architects to harmonise with the natural features of the country. Not often on the French and Belgian sites has it been possible to attain the supreme loveliness of some of the Italian cemeteries, but all are beautiful. The first British burial took place in the Warloy-Baillon Communal Cemetery in October 1915, and the last on July 1st 1916. By that date field ambulances had come to the village in readiness for the attack on the German line, five miles away, and the Extension was begun. There are buried in the Extension 857 soldiers from the Home Country, 318 from Australia, 152 from Canada, and 3 unknown. The Communal Cemetery records 46 British burials.

FORCEVILLE. This cemetery is to the west of the village of Forceville, about twelve miles from Doullens and six miles from Albert. In 1915 British troops of the Third Army took over the area from the French. In February 1916 a field ambulance was established in the village, and it was followed by others until the end of July 1916. Early in August 1915 additional land to the south of the Communal Cemetery was enclosed to provide space for military graves. This land is enclosed by a low wall and a hedge. Some of the old poplar trees have been preserved and fragrant lime trees planted (the lime-tree avenues of Amiens will be recalled by the troops on whom they showered their perfume as they went forward for the first Battle of the Somme).

LOUVENCOURT. The Military Cemetery here is south-east of the village, which is midway between Albert and Doullens. The French soldiers' graves dated June and July 1915 mark the end of the French occupation of the Allied front on the Somme. The British graves cover the period from July 1915 to July 1918. Louvencourt Military Cemetery is enclosed by a great stone wall and the paths are stone paved. The Cross of Sacrifice is placed at the entrance. The Stone of Remembrance is at the east side of the cemetery, and the steps of it command a wide view over the north country. The cemetery holds 151 British dead.

PICQUIGNY. There are here a communal cemetery and a British military cemetery. The historic town (where a treaty of peace between France and England was signed in 1475) lies in the valley of the Somme River, on the main road between Abbeville and Amiens. During the first four years of the war Picquigny was on lines of communication, and the ten British soldiers who died in or near the town were buried in the Communal Cemetery. At the end of March 1918 casualty-clearing stations were brought to Picquigny, and the British Cemetery was opened a little west of the town. It shelters 94 soldiers from the Home Country, 29 from Australia, one from Canada and one unknown, and one French soldier.

CROUY. The British Cemetery here is about half a mile south of the village, near the Amiens-Abbeville main road. It was opened in April 1918 when the enemy advance sent two casualty-clearing stations to the village. In October 1919 the graves from the British Cemetery at Rivière, a few miles nearer Abbeville, were brought to Crouy. There are now buried in Crouy 281 soldiers from the Home Country, 275 from Australia, 179 from Canada and one of the British West Indies Regiment, 2 labourers of the Indian Labour Corps, and 6 French soldiers.

LONGPRÉ-LES-CORPS SAINTS. The village owes its name to relics sent from the Holy Land by the founder of the church in the twelfth century. In April 1918 there was opened a British cemetery. It was closed before the end of the month, and the present cemetery opened about half a mile south of the village. In May 1919 the graves from the first cemetery were moved to it. The cemetery now contains 56 British graves, 20 Australians, and one French.

◆   ◆   ◆   ◆   ◆

On this day, during the morning and afternoon, the only bad weather occurred, but the rainstorms did not in any way deter the King from carrying out the programme which he had determined on. At all the cemeteries visited in the afternoon there were striking demonstrations of affection by the country people. The smaller cemeteries were surrounded by the villagers, five or six deep, the children standing on the low walls, the King as he inspected the graves passing close to them. All maintained an attitude of sympathetic reverence. The King, who was evidently moved, showed on many occasions how he felt himself among friends and was visibly interested in the little children who stared round-eyed at "the King of the British soldiers."

As the train steamed into Picquigny Station, the Bishop of Amiens was seen standing with his clergy on the platform, having come out from Amiens, specially and without interfering with the privacy of the pilgrimage, sympathetically to greet our King. The Bishop reminded His Majesty that the last time a King of England had come to Picquigny was in 1475, when Edward IV agreed there on a treaty of peace with the French King. King George V must have been interested to remember the piquant contrast between then and now, for when in 1475 Edward met Louis at Picquigny a close fence was built across a bridge "with no longer intervals than would allow the arm to pass," and the two kings came from opposite sides to meet and confer under those precautions of mistrust. Now a British King moved among the people of France with no guard but their respect and love for him and his Army.

ÉTAPLES

INSPECTING SOUTH AFRICAN GRAVES

ÉTAPLES

INSPECTING NEWFOUNDLAND GRAVES

ÉTAPLES

THE KING READING THE LETTER FROM A BEREAVED
MOTHER ASKING THE QUEEN TO PLACE A BUNCH OF
FORGET-ME-NOTS ON HER SON'S GRAVE

ÉTAPLES

THE KING PLACING THE FORGET-ME-NOTS ON THE GRAVE

ÉTAPLES

AT THE STONE OF REMEMBRANCE

GENERAL VIEW OF ÉTAPLES

THE KING AND DOMINION REPRESENTATIVES

ÉTAPLES

EXAMINING PLANS OF CONSTRUCTION WORK

TERLINCTHUN: THE LAST POST

"They lie in the keeping of a tried and generous friend, a resolute and chivalrous comrade-in-arms, who, with ready and quick sympathy, has set aside for ever the soil in which they sleep, so that we ourselves and our descendants may for all time reverently tend and preserve their resting-places."

MEERUT INDIAN CEMETERY

INSPECTING INDIAN GRAVES

TERLINCTHUN

THE FRENCH GUARD OF HONOUR AT THE CROSS OF SACRIFICE

TERLINCTHUN

THE KING PLACING A WREATH ON THE CROSS OF SACRIFICE

TERLINCTHUN

THE SILENCE AND THE SALUTE AT THE CROSS

TERLINCTHUN

THE KING'S ADDRESS

"And the last land he found it was fair and level ground
About a carven stone,
And a stark sword brooding on the bosom of the cross
Where high and low are one."

TERLINCTHUN

GENERAL DE CASTELNAU'S REPLY

TERLINCTHUN

PROCESSION TO THE STONE OF REMEMBRANCE

TERLINCTHUN

PROCESSION TO THE STONE OF REMEMBRANCE

"All that they had they gave – they gave"

TERLINCTHUN

THE QUEEN LAYING A WREATH ON
THE STONE OF REMEMBRANCE

TERLINCTHUN

THE SALUTE AT THE STONE OF REMEMBRANCE

TERLINCTHUN

THE QUEEN AT THE GRAVES

TERLINCTHUN

THE QUEEN AT THE GRAVES

TERLINCTHUN

THE STONE OF REMEMBRANCE WITH THE QUEEN'S WREATH

"Their name liveth for evermore"

TERLINCTHUN

NAPOLEON'S COLUMN IN THE BACKGROUND

*"And here ... the shadow of his monument falling
almost across their graves, the greatest of French soldiers
– of all soldiers – stands guard over them"*

LEAVING ÉTAPLES

"In the course of my pilgrimage I have many times asked myself whether there can be more potent advocates of peace upon earth through the years to come than this massed multitude of silent witnesses to the desolation of war"

ON the evening of May 12th the King's train left Longpré and went down to the coast. The night was spent at Étaples, a fishing port at the mouth of the River Canche, which has figured since many centuries back in the history of the British Empire, and now is the site of what has come to be known as our "Empire Cemetery" in France.

When the Romans were bringing in the path of their legions order and civilization into Europe – misfortunately thwarted by forest or bog or sea from reaching some countries, which have suffered from the fact since – they had their chief naval station for northern Gaul at the mouth of the Canche. This station, no doubt, Julius Caesar used in his expedition against Britain. Later, when Carausius, a Roman Briton, revolted against the Roman Empire, he won the command of the English Channel with his fleet and maintained for some time an independent Britain, assuming the state of Caesar and founding a Roman-British Empire. The *Classis Britannica* of the Roman Empire had had its chief station on the Canche. With the revolt of Carausius there was no longer a "British Fleet" of the Roman Empire, and the *Classis Samarica* (the Fleet of the Somme) took its place and had as its task to hold the coasts of Gaul for the Roman Power against the British Carausius. This Fleet of the Somme also had its

base on the Canche. Doubtless in the very early years of
the Christian era there was many a naval action between
the British sea forces and those of the Romans stationed
on the Canche. Étaples is thus linked with the memory of
Carausius, the man who first taught England that her fate
depended on the holding of the Narrow Seas.

Étaples during the Great War was for long our chief
hospital centre. In the middle of the coast base line,
having good railway communications with most points,
within sight and smell of the sea, the sand dunes around
Étaples were ideal for hospital hutments. To the Étaples
hospitals there came wounded from every battlefield. To
them there came also in 1918 the attacking air squadrons
of the enemy, which accounts in part for the number of
nurses and other medical personnel buried in Étaples
Cemetery. One hospital at Étaples was set on fire and
destroyed by the enemy. These aircraft attacks on the
Étaples hospitals came in June 1918, when the enemy
concentrated his strategy on trying to cripple our means
of supply. They inflicted grave embarrassment on our High
Command, for, at a time when material was very scanty
and lines of transport very congested, we had to construct
new hospitals elsewhere and move patients and staff. That
was probably the effect aimed at. The difference, from an
enemy point of view, in bombing a camp and a hospital
is this: If you bomb a camp, you kill a few men, but the
camp does not move; if you bomb a hospital, you kill a few
patients, nurses, and doctors, and you force the hospital to
move (if it can move) to a safer place. But to the end of the
war some hospitals remained because it was impossible to
move them.

In 1917 the hospitals at Étaples (which included eleven

general, one stationary, and four Red Cross hospitals and a convalescent depot) could deal with 22,000 wounded or sick. The earliest burial in the cemetery dates from May 1915. The graves today number more than 11,000. Of these, 1,984 were from the Overseas Dominions, divided as follows: Canada, 1,122; Australia, 461; New Zealand, 261; South Africa, 67; West Indies, 29; India, 26; and Newfoundland, 18.

The site of Étaples Cemetery is very beautiful. It rises from the margin of the sea in three great terraces, in the middle one of which is the Stone of Remembrance and on the highest the Cross of Sacrifice, standing up stark against a grove of pine trees. From the cemetery the valley of the Canche flows up to the walls of Montreuil-sur-Mer, which was the General Headquarters of the British Army from 1916 until the close of the war.

It was early when the King arrived at Étaples Cemetery. The sea was a soft flood of silver grey in the morning light, and its salt breath, which is the very vigour of our British blood, came up sharp and strong to meet the smell of the pines, which is the smell of a ship's cordage. A seemly place for the graves of a sailor race.

Outside the gates of Étaples Cemetery, the Mayor of Étaples and the sub-prefect of Montreuil greeted the King, and there were presented to him French veterans of the Great War and of the war of 1870. The King remained a few moments talking with them and with two Anzac motor drivers, who are of the very small band of the Australian Army Corps still remaining in France. The King had expressed the wish that at this cemetery he should meet representatives of the Dominions and visit with them the graves of their fellow-countrymen.

Accordingly, on entering the cemetery, the King was met by the Hon. P. C. Larkin, High Commissioner for Canada; Sir James Allen, High Commissioner for New Zealand; Sir Edgar Bowring, High Commissioner for Newfoundland; Lieutenant-Colonel G. J. Hogben and Colonel F. R. Collins, representing Australia and South Africa respectively in the absence of their High Commissioners at the Genoa Conference. With each of these in turn the King visited the graves of their Dominions, and spoke to them in proud appreciation of the gallant aid that the children nations of the Empire had given to the Mother Country. That this Imperial Cemetery should stand by the side of the sea, the communicating bond of the world-girdling British race, was referred to as the fitting thing.

Before leaving, the King showed, by an act of simple homage at the grave of a soldier, his feeling of kinship with those comrades of his who had fallen in the war. A woman in the West of England had written to the Queen, as one mother to another, begging that she might lay on the tomb of her dead son, Sergeant Matthew, R.A.S.C., in Étaples Cemetery, a spray of forget-me-nots which she enclosed. The Queen was unable to be present (she arrived later from Belgium), but confided the mission to the King. He had brought with him the letter, and carried out reverently, dutifully the pious task, taking care, accompanied by Mr. Harry Gosling and the gardener, to find the grave and, bending down in homage, to place upon it the mother's flowers. Standing by his side was Sir James Allen, the High Commissioner for New Zealand, who had lost a son in Gallipoli.

Going up, then, to the Cross of Sacrifice, the King looked long out over the marshalled graves to the sea, and turned back towards the pine wood which encloses the cemetery on the east. From Étaples Cemetery the King and his party returned to the train, and then proceeded along the coastline to Wimereux Station, where they again took car and visited Meerut Cemetery, which commemorates the devotion of India to the King Emperor. Here rest men of every rank and every caste and every race of India who crossed the black water to fight for their Emperor. This cemetery, austere, remote, dark cypresses breaking the line of its turf, with no flower nor Western symbol of remembrance and hope, records the British respect for whatever form the aspiration towards God takes in the human heart.

The King was met by General Sir Alexander Cobbe, V.C., representing the Secretary of State for India, and the Mayor of the Commune of St. Martin, in which commune the cemetery is situated. It was pointed out to the King that some 330 native soldiers and followers were commemorated after the disposition of their bodies according to their creeds. The headstones had been erected by the Indian Soldiers' Fund, the walls around the cemetery by the War Office.

The King inquired as to a central memorial in the cemetery, and was told that probably a Great War stone would be erected in the centre, and that in erecting headstones where required the War Graves Commission would follow the same pattern as already existed in the cemetery. He suggested that the crematorium might be now removed, and showed in other ways his deep interest that all the sentiments should be respected of the kinfolk of these men, of race and religion apart from our own but united to us in the bond of a common sacrifice.

◆　　◆　　◆　　◆　　◆

Now had come the last stage of the King's pilgrimage. Already outside the port of Boulogne there was assembled a squadron of French destroyers to escort him out of French waters, and further at sea a British squadron waited to take over the guard. For all that their task today was to be one of honour and ceremony, they could abate nothing of that eager, crouching-forward attitude, and they seemed to sniff at every wave for a submarine. They waited, hunters become courtiers, but the King for a time turned his back to them, his duty not yet accomplished. He had seen the graves of his sailors, soldiers, and airmen who had held to their trust by sea and land and air, from the gates of Ypres to the banks of the Somme; had mourned at their loss and had thrilled with the pride of their courage. Now he went his way to the high Terlincthun Cemetery, by Napoleon's column on the Boulogne cliffs, to say to his people what was in his mind.

Of all the war cemeteries in France there is none more nobly planned than this of Terlincthun. It is set at the foot of Napoleon's column, where rested the right wing of the Grand Army when its face was turned towards England. But the guardian sea lay between. It is on record that there was offered to France a plan of conquering the Channel passage by the use of submarine boats; and refused on the ground that the sentiment of humanity would not tolerate the use of such a weapon even against warships. "It seems impossible," wrote the French Minister for Marine, Admiral Pléville de Pelley in 1801, "to serve a commission as belligerents to men who employ such a method of destroying the fleets of the enemy." The British dead can rest content and comradely beneath the monument of so gallant a foe.

From its high wind-swept cliff, Terlincthun Cemetery looks over the English Channel, and on a clear day the white cliffs of our coast shine out in the distance. The Stone of Remembrance faces towards home, the Cross of Sacrifice, bearing its great bronze sword, looks towards the old enemy lines. Between, like guardian walls, are ranked the lines of gravestones, and around them flowerbeds carpeted in this season with the foliage of wallflowers. Happy was the choice of this flower for a soldiers' graveyard, since it loves to spread its tapestry of gold and red over ramparts. The cemetery shelters 3,327 dead. They are in almost all cases men who died at the base hospitals at Boulogne and Wimereux. But some are the bodies of British seamen washed up on the coast and buried here. Many graves are of Royal Air Force members. The graves of the Empire dead number 2,551 of the Home Country, 277 Canadian, 88 Australian, 29 New Zealand, 10 Newfoundland, one South African, one Guernsey, 33 South African Native, and 5 West Indian Native. In addition, there are 92 American graves, 27 Italian, 4 Russian, 3 Polish, 2 Serbian, and 16 of unknown nationality.

For this, the crowning act of homage, the King was joined by the Queen, who had travelled that morning from Brussels. With the Royal party were Admiral the Earl Beatty and Field-Marshal the Earl Haig (who jointly represented the Navy, the Army, and the Air Force). At the gate of the cemetery the King and Queen were received by General de Castelnau, representing the French Army; M. Cauzel, prefect of the Departement of Pas-de-Calais; Admiral Barthes, naval prefect of Cherbourg; General

Lacapelle, commanding the First Army Corps; General Philippeau, commanding the Second Army Corps; Mgr. Julien, Bishop of Arras; M. de Lavergne, K.B.E.; M. Lahan, sub-prefect of Boulogne; the Mayor of Boulogne, and other French officials, and the members of the Imperial War Graves Commission, whom it was His Majesty's expressed desire to meet at the close of his pilgrimage. Mr. Herbert Baker, the architect who designed the cemetery, and Captain A. W. Hill, D.Sc, were also present. Among the French officials was M. Le Sous-Intendant Bezombes, C.B.E., who is the administrative head of the French Government services dealing with their own war graves. All who realise the extent of the French losses can understand what a tremendous task falls to him; but he has never been too busy to help our Commission in overcoming any of their difficulties. One of the first acts of the King, after his arrival, was to express to M. Bezombes and his staff the deep and sincere gratitude of the British Empire for their ungrudging support and sympathy in this work. The citizens of Boulogne had assembled around the cemetery and gave the King and Queen a cordial greeting. Within the open space before the Cross of Sacrifice were gathered many relatives of the dead, members of the British Colony and of the staff of the Imperial War Graves Commission, and a number of French sympathisers.

King George and Queen Mary, passing through an aisle between the serried ranks of graves, advanced to the Cross of Sacrifice, and the King placed at its foot his chaplet of red roses, palms, and bay, and stood at the salute. The French Guard of Honour, clean, clear-cut figures in their helmets of classic line, recalling the Roman Legionaries, came to the salute, and for two hushed minutes, even as our whole realm stands for two minutes on each 11th of November, all thoughts were given up to the memory of the dead.

Still standing at the Cross of Sacrifice, the King turned his face then towards the Stone of Remembrance, both in direct alignment with Napoleon's Column, which closed the perspective, and, his voice vibrant with emotion, but under rigid control, delivered his message to his people over all the seas, in the name of the Queen and of himself:

> For the past few days I have been on a solemn pilgrimage in honour of a people who died for all free men.
>
> At the close of that pilgrimage, on which I followed ways already marked by many footsteps of love and pride and grief, I should like to send a message to all who have lost those dear to them in the Great War, and in this the Queen joins me today, amidst these surroundings so wonderfully typical of that single-hearted assembly of nations and of races which form our Empire. For here, in their last quarters, lie sons of every portion of that Empire, across, as it were, the threshold of the Mother Island which they guarded that Freedom might be saved in the uttermost ends of the earth.
>
> For this, a generation of our manhood offered itself without question, and almost without the need of a summons. Those proofs of virtue, which we honour here today, are to be found throughout the world and its waters – since we can truly say that the whole circuit of the earth is girdled with the graves of our dead. Beyond the stately cemeteries of France, across Italy, through Eastern Europe in wellnigh unbroken chain they stretch, passing over the holy mount of Olives itself to the farthest shores of the Indian and Pacific Oceans – from Zeebrugge to Coronel, from Dunkirk to the hidden wildernesses of East Africa.
>
> But in this fair land of France, which sustained the utmost fury of the long strife, our brothers are numbered, alas! by hundreds of thousands. They lie in the keeping of a tried

and generous friend, a resolute and chivalrous comrade-in-arms, who with ready and quick sympathy has set aside for ever the soil in which they sleep, so that we ourselves and our descendants may for all time reverently tend and preserve their resting-places. And here, at Terlincthun, the shadow of his monument falling almost across their graves, the greatest of French soldiers – of all soldiers – stands guard over them. And this is just, for, side by side with the descendants of his incomparable armies, they defended his land in defending their own.

Never before in history have a people thus dedicated and maintained individual memorials to their fallen, and, in the course of my pilgrimage, I have many times asked myself whether there can be more potent advocates of peace upon earth through the years to come, than this massed multitude of silent witnesses to the desolation of war. And I feel that, so long as we have faith in God's purposes, we cannot but believe that the existence of these visible memorials will, eventually, serve to draw all peoples together in sanity and self-control, even as it has already set the relations between our Empire and our allies on the deep-rooted bases of a common heroism and a common agony.

Standing beneath this Cross of Sacrifice, facing the great Stone of Remembrance, and compassed by these sternly simple headstones, we remember, and must charge our children to remember, that, as our dead were equal in sacrifice, so are they equal in honour, for the greatest and the least of them have proved that sacrifice and honour are no vain things, but truths by which the world lives.

Many of the cemeteries I have visited in the remoter and still desolate districts of this sorely stricken land, where, it has not yet been possible to re-place the wooden crosses by headstones, have been made into beautiful gardens which are lovingly cared for by comrades of the war. I rejoice I was fortunate enough to see these in the spring, when the returning pulse of the year tells of unbroken life that goes forward in the face of apparent loss and wreckage; and I fervently pray that, both as nations and individuals, we may so order our lives after the ideals for which our brethren died, that we may be able to meet their gallant souls once more, humbly but unashamed.

General de Castelnau responded with like eloquence and feeling. Two sentences of his reply voiced a sacred pledge:

> Nous garderons religieusement le dépôt sacré confié à notre dévotion, ici, à Terlincthun, comme dans toutes les nécropoles du front qui, de Boulogne à Belfort, jalonnent dans un funèbre alignement la voie sacrée, le calvaire des souffrances, des agonies et des deuils gravi la main dans la main par les valeureux combattants de nos deux nations.
>
> Et lorsque chargé des parfums de la Patrie toute proche, le vent du large apportera à ces tombes la douce caresse du foyer natal, il se confondra avec le souffle de piété tendre et fidèle dont sont pénétrés toutes les âmes et tous les cœurs français pour les héros de l'Angleterre et de la France qui, tombés côté à côté au champ d'honneur, dorment côté à côté à l'ombre d'austères forêts de croix de bois élevant vers le Ciel leurs bras de miséricorde et d'espérance.

General de Castelnau then laid at the foot of the Cross of Sacrifice a wreath in the name of the Anglo-French Committee of our War Graves Commission, and General Lacapelle another in the name of the French Army.

One more act of homage was to be made. The King and Queen, passing slowly through the cemetery, ascended the steps to the Stone of Remembrance and then, bending lowly, the Queen placed before the stone, over which was draped the Union Jack – the merited pall of a soldier's tomb – a wreath of rosemary for remembrance, and carnations, these last of the colour which takes its name from the stricken battlefield of Magenta. The French Guard of Honour saluted, lowering their standard. Its colours, mingled with the colours of our flag and with the deep purple of the Queen's tribute, suffused the white stone as with heroes' blood. The King and those around him saluted, while from the bugles of the Coldstream and Grenadier Guards, posted near the Great Napoleon's Column, there came the sound, as of a long-drawn-out sigh, of "The Last Post".

There is no music, of all the music of the world, that so brings home to the soldier's heart, proud sorrow, healing consolation. In the daily round of his dutiful work, "The Last Post" comes to tell him of the end of a day of this troublous life, that the shades have lengthened, the evening come, the busy world hushed, his work done, and he may rest. And, when he goes to the graveside to say the last farewell to a comrade who has found for ever peace, he hears again "The Last Post", to say to him that his mate is not dead, but sleepeth, and will rise again. The common and everyday use of the music takes nothing from its nobility, but constantly communicates its message of immortality so as to make of it a habit of mind.

The call of "The Last Post" ended; and to the closing moment of the King's pilgrimage came a sense of overpowering emotion, which made men look resolutely forward, not wishing to catch their neighbour's glance. The spirits of the mighty army of the dead seemed to marshall in that God's Acre, set high on the cliff looking over the sea; come to receive the homage of the King, for whom they died, and to hear that in the land which they saved their names will live for evermore.

FRANK FOX

The King's Thanks

On the point of leaving France, the King sent the following telegram to the President of the French Republic:

> I have today brought to an end a visit to the graves of my countrymen who gave their lives on the battlefields of France, and now lie covered by the same blood-stained soil as, alas! so many of their heroic French brothers-in-arms.
>
> Before leaving Boulogne, I desire, Monsieur le President, to send to you from a full heart, and speaking in the name of all the people of my Empire, a message of profound gratitude for the generous gift of the ground for ever hallowed by the memories of common sorrows and glories. These memories must recall for all time the sentiment of faithful comradeship which inspired those who fell side by side in the Great War, and which was bequeathed by them as a sacred legacy to our two nations.
>
> I would add an expression of my personal thanks to you, Monsieur le President, and to the French people, among whom I have spent these three days, for the touching sympathy with my desire to make this pilgrimage in such privacy as was in harmony with my feeling of reverent affection for the dead and respect for those to whom they are dear.

The following message was sent to the King of the Belgians:

> ... May I add how touched I was by the sympathetic attitude of all classes whom I met last Thursday, when visiting the graves of our dead resting for ever on Belgian soil.

The King later caused the following letter to be sent to the Vice-Chairman of the Imperial War Graves Commission:

BUCKINGHAM PALACE,
May 17, 1922.

DEAR SIR FABIAN WARE,

The King desires me to thank you again for all the admirable arrangements made by your connection with the visit to the cemeteries in Belgium and France and to congratulate your staff on their excellent work. His Majesty was interested to learn the details of the organisation of the Commission, and is satisfied that, so long as it is superintended by you and those who so loyally assist you, the public here and Overseas can rest assured that the graves, wherever they may be, will be properly cared for.

The King hopes you will take an opportunity of telling the members of the Imperial War Graves Commission how much he appreciated their presence at the ceremony at Terlincthun.* His Majesty also wishes you to say that he trusts the High Commissioner and other representatives of the Dominions will convey to their Governments and people the great

---

* The following are the members of the Imperial War Graves Commission, those marked with a † being unavoidably prevented, owing to the Genoa Conference and other reasons, from personally attending: † Secretary of State for War (Chairman), † Secretary of State for the Colonies, † Secretary of State for India, † First Commissioner of Works, The Hon. Peter C. Larkin (High Commissioner for Canada), † The Right Hon. Sir Joseph Cook, G.C.M.G. (High Commissioner for Australia), The Hon. Sir James Allen, K.C.B. (High Commissioner for New Zealand), † The Hon. Sir Edgar Walton, K.C.M.G. (High Commissioner for the Union of South Africa), The Hon. Sir Edgar Bowring (High Commissioner for Newfoundland), Sir William Garstin, G.C.M.G., G.B.E., Harry Gosling, Esq., C.H., J.P., Rudyard Kipling, Esq., Lieutenant-General Sir George Macdonogh, K.C.B., K.C.M.G., Sir Robert Hudson, G.B.E., Vice-Admiral Sir Morgan Singer, K.C.V.O., C.B., † H. Maddocks, Esq., K.C., M.P., Major-General Sir Fabian Ware, K.C.V.O., K.B.E., C.B., C.M.G. (Vice-Chairman).

satisfaction he expressed to them personally at Étaples at the care bestowed by the Commission on the graves of those who are so far from their homes. In all the cemeteries visited by His Majesty, Dominion and British graves lay side by side, and the King assures the people Overseas that these graves will be reverently and lovingly guarded. It is a satisfaction to His Majesty that the Imperial War Graves Commission has been so constituted that these graves may be honoured for all time.

The King was impressed by the ability and efficiency of the gardeners in the service of the Commission, and desires that his appreciation may be expressed to them of the manner in which they carry out their precious charge. Although the completion of these cemeteries must necessarily take some time, especially in the still-devastated areas, they may continue their work with the full conviction that they are earning the deep gratitude of the relatives and friends of those whose graves they tend.

Yours sincerely,
F. E. G. PONSONBY

The High Commissioners cabled to the Governments and peoples of the Dominions the terms of the King's assurance that the graves of their dead will be honoured for all time.